Prog II

By

John F King

Prog II

Featuring Morris Spiegelman

'….If we want to know, we must listen - on a still June night, by preference, with the breathing of the invisible sea for background to the music and scent of lime trees drifting through the darkness, like some exquisite soft harmony apprehended by another sense.'

A Huxley *Music at Night*

Prog 11 part 1 -

Morris Spiegelman is Alright

By

John F King

A new audio drama 2023

York Europe Publications

ISBN 978-1-8383426-3-0

                                    PRELUDE

EXT

ACOUSTIC

—

EVENING

MASSIVE STADIUM, CROWD, MORRIS AND DEZ HIT IN FULL FLOW, THEY SPEAK THROUGH THE APPLAUSE

MORRIS
London, we love you

DEZ
Beautiful, thank you, people

MORE MUSIC, APPLAUSE

MORRIS
Vienna, wir lieben Sie, we love music, we love you…

Copenhagen, so wonderful, I promise we'll be back

…

DEZ THROUGH THE APPLAUSE TO MORRIS We made it man, we made it , the music, the life, we made it

MORE MUSIC, APPLAUSE   MORRIS   New York, New York, we love you twice, we…we..

DEZ ON STAGE ASIDE
Morris, Morris, you cool, man? Morris…!

SILENCE

1 INT to EXT

CHERWELL MANOR,

A SPRING

MORNING THROUGH THE

OFFICE WINDOW BIRD SONG, RUSTLE OF TREES, FOUNTAIN

DOOR OPENS AND CLOSES, DOC BEGINS WALKING FROM HER OFFICE ALONG CORRIDOR TO EXTERNAL DOOR, OPENS, SPRING SOUNDS INTENSIFY, PEACEFUL, DOC TAKES A DEEP BREATH WALKING ACROSS GRAVEL DRIVE

EXT

DOC

You can tell so much - not everything - about people by the way they arrive here. Noisy, quiet, flamboyant, apologetic, I have a right to be here, I hate being here, I was sent, I belong here, I'm not really here.

Please allow me to introduce myself. Doctor Ingrid Voss, leader of rehabilitation programmes, Cherwell Manor or to give the place it's proper title…

AS SHE IS SPEAKING THE TRANQUIL BACKGROUND IS OVERWHELMED BY THE ROAR OF SUPERCARS

…Cherwell Manor, centre for rehabilitation, recreation and reconciliation…

HER SPEECH TEMPORARILY LOST AS CARS ROAR UP THE GRAVEL DRIVE

…recreation in the sense of recreating who you are, reconciliation with yourself.

SPRING SILENCE RETURNS

Naturally approaches have changed since I first started my practice at Cherwell Manor. Some things change, some remain the same.

Then everyone arrived in Astons, Bentleys, Jensens, no exceptions. Rehab. It was an inverse boast, a rite, fast cars, helicopters, exemplify your own myth, drugs. MOTOR SOUNDS BULDING AGAIN AN APPROACHING HELICOPTER, DOC RESUMES AFTER IT LANDS,

Yes, drugs, who are you without them, do you want to face that?

I make no judgement how and why people come here.

SPRING SILENCE RETURNS, THROUGH THE RUSTLE OF TREES AND BIRDSONG THE SOUND OF AN APPROACHING BICYLE

Looking back I can understand it was inevitable the way Morris Spiegelman arrived…by bicycle. You will appreciate that what happens next, within the Manor and our grounds is confidential.

RING OF BICYCLE BELL, IT PEDALS TO A HALT.

DIRECTOR
Welcome to the institute, Mr Spiegelman. I am the Director. I have heard so much about you.

MORRIS
An institutional director who has heard about me, don't make me feel I made the wrong choice before I've even got off my bicycle

DIRECTOR
Dr Voss will be in charge.

Don't take this the wrong way Mr Spiegelman, it is a delight to meet you but I hope I never see you again. Dr Voss. Yours.

DOC
Good morning

MORRIS
Hello. Honey.

DOC
I prefer doctor.

MORRIS
You want to know why I am here.   Honey. Manuka. I spent all my royalties on honey. I expect you will want me to be open. I mixed in cocaine and alcohol.

DOC
Mr Spiegelman, Morris if I may? Welcome to Cherwell Manor.

MORRIS
Do you know how much these substances are, what they cost me?

DOC
Manuka, Cocaine, Alcohol? Would you like to tell me?
Let's have a walk first, house or grounds?
THEY CRUNCH OFF THE GRAVEL DRIVE.

2

INT – THE NEXT MORNING IN DR VOSS CONSULTING ROOM. SHE IS WRITING HER NOTES, WINDOW OPEN. A HELICOPTER ARRIVES. SHE DOESN'T HEAR KNOCK AT DOOR. SHE CLOSES WINDOW. OUTSIDE NOISE SUBSIDES.
KNOCK AGAIN.

DOC
Come

MORRIS
Can't you hear me knocking? I don't dig being ignored, kept waiting…
THERE IS NO APOLOGY

DOC
Mr Spiegelman, come in, please sit where you like, window open or closed? I hope you had a pleasant evening and breakfast and are enjoying our facilities.   Formalities first.
Names? Mr Spiegelman, Morris, I have researched your stage name, Moz?

MORRIS
Morris.

DOC
Morris. As I said yesterday my name is Doctor Ingrid Voss, I am in charge of your programme here at Cherwell Manor..

3

INT – THE NEXT DAY, DOC'S CONSULTING ROOM. TEA WITH HONEY SERVED

DOC

Is the tea to your taste, Morris?
Do you want to tell me about your evening?

MORRIS

Questions, questions. What do you want me to say?

DOC

Do you want to be here, Morris? You can leave any time, there are no walls.

MORRIS

Physically

DOC

What is it you want to tell me, Morris?

MORRIS

What do you want to know, is there something you need me to tell you so you can tell me to leave?

DOC

I'm listening. I'm not hearing anything.

MORRIS

I expect all you are interested in is drugs.

DOC

Drugs are of no intrinsic interest to me. You have brought up the subject of what you refer to as drugs. I never asked you. I'll listen to whatever you want to air.

MORRIS

On air, on drugs, that's clever, Doc, brings us to today's subject neatly.

DOC

I'm listening.

ACOUSTIC CHANGES TO INT OF A RADIO STUDIO.

RADIO JINGLE. DEMO OF DEZ AND MORRIS SINGLE PLAYING IN BACKGROUND.

MORRIS

V/O

Even before graduation, we'd blagged it into a radio studio…

RADIO STATION JINGLE

DJ

People, one day in the not too distant future there will be a stadium big enough for that mega hit, speaking of the future live in the studio with me today are two young men – what is the plural of genius? – yes, the future is here today, it's Morris 'Moz' and Dez or is that Dez and Moz, who cares, fellas welcome.

DEZ

What's happening, man

MORRIS

Good afternoon

DJ

It's all happening here live this afternoon. Listen, talk is easy, let's get down to it, music, here it is , the latest, or is that the first, I hope it is not the only from Moz and Dez, 'Most Definitely':

PLAYS SONG

DJ TALKS TO MORRIS AND DEZ WHILE THEIR (PRE-HELEN)DEMO IS BROADCAST

It works like this – end of
your demo, bantz, new plans
etc, keep it light and
tight, about 4 mins, out
and back to playlist,
yeah?

MORRIS

It's Morris not Moz, and I don't think it's a demo.

DEZ

It's cool

DJ

Whatever you say fellas. Less tech more music.

MORRIS
If you don't like what we do why don't you...
THE MUSIC IS STILL PLAYING

DJ
I can't wait for the vocal to kick in.

DEZ
We're on it, right Moz?
MUSIC FADE DOWN

DJ
People we are back live with Moz and Dez, one day these dudes will be the future, right now let's chat.
Moz, love the track, look forward to the vocal, how is that coming?

MORRIS
The vocal line is right up there with the synclavier and I said call me Mor...

DEZ
People, Moz and Dez love this show, dream come true, great to be here.

DJ
We love you too, Dez. We'll be right back after this.   JINGLE

INT - CONSULTING ROOM

DOC
What occurred next?

MORRIS
TAKES GULP OF TEA AND CONTINUES   George Lennox happened next. Same university year as us, Dez, Helen and I but he was studying politics.
We were leaving the radio station, he was in the studio next door.
BACK IN THE STUDIO CORRIDOR

GEORGE
Pushing the merchandise, Moz?

MORRIS
You don't call me Moz

GEORGE
Stirring sound but clearly he has a point about the vocal.

MORRIS
What are you doing here, Lennox. Never knew you were into music.

GEORGE
I was in the studio next door, Moz, feature on most promising newcomers. In politics.

MORRIS
So why are you on it?

GEORGE

Future PM someone said. Who am I to disagree. Politics, music, obs this stage you have to play the game, Moz. Dez, Helen, me, we're naturals. You, my good man, need to loosen up. Bantz. Look, why don't you try one of these next time you go on air? If there is a next time. Have this one on the house.

MORRIS

What is it?

GEORGE

Try it. You'll be a different person. Everyone will like you.

HE MIMICS MORRIS Good afternoon.

ACOUSTIC BACK TO DOC CONSULTING ROOM

DOC

You take things you are offered without question?

MORRIS

Your point?

DOC

You are here because the drugs don't work, never did, or don't any more?

MORRIS

You tell me, Doctor

DOC

Why don't you ask some questions?

4
INT – THE NEXT DAY

DOC
Morris, are you exploring the facilities here, the grounds, the library, the pool, the common room, interacting with any of our other guests?

MORRIS
Guests? No. Why would I?

DOC
There are others here, people of interest, people with experiences, artistes, musicians…I would prefer you not to use your computer when we are talking. Please?

MORRIS
It's a workstation. You are talking. Laptop OPENS Listen. The DJ was right. This is the magic HELEN VOCAL We were ..

DOC
Were ?

MORRIS
..we were a trio. Not a duo. Greater than the sum of the parts. The DJ heard right. The vocal, Helen's vocal, gives it – us – life. That is why we had the hit. That's how it all went right.

MORRIS

What do I call you? Doc, Ingrid..

DOC

Are names important to you, Morris? Do you want me to decide for you?

Some basics. Everything that happens in this room, in this manor is confidential.

MORRIS

I'm sure you have heard everything before, rock and roll people, showbiz kids, politicos, I'm not really interested in other people right now.

DOC

What are you interested in Morris. Honey. With tea?

SHE PROVIDES TWO CUPS OF TEA. THEY STIR IN THE HONEY.

SILENCE

DOC SIPS TEA AND OPENS WINDOW

MORRIS

Do you always do that or is that part of my programme?...asking me do you want the window open or closed and opening it anyway.

DOC

Why don't we start?

MORRIS

Yeah. Where?

DOC
The beginning? Your timeline, Morris. Morris?

MORRIS
I'll start at the beginning, Doc. Maybe that's how it ended.
FX REVERB OF ROCK MUSIC KEYBOARD / GUITAR DISTORTION TO- INT YEARS EARLIER , A STUDENT ROOM AT LEEDS UNIVERSITY HALL OF RESIDENCE
MORRIS V/O ABOVE MUSICAL INSTRUMENTS PLAYED FROM LAPTOPS
We were a duo first, a trio second. I liked the beginning best. Me and Dez, inseparable in sound, I knew we had something, we didn't know how far it would go, you don't think that far ahead at that age do you …?

DEZ AND MORRIS ARE IMPROVISING ON THEIR LAPTOPS/ INSTRUMENTS
DEZ
Yeah, cool, liking it, E minor

MORRIS
Keep it major, E7 progression to

DEZ
Bridge. Nice

MORRIS
Stay on it. G

DEZ
G13

MORRIS
We need something. Sounds like two guys studying music tech at Leeds Met. Proud of that, but…

DEZ
Chorus. Hook.

MORRIS
Synth, Vocal?
It's kind of almost

DEZ
I feel you, bro. Get this.
MORE RIFFS, CHORDS, AT FIRST THEY DON'T HEAR DOOR KNOCK

MORRIS
There is someone at the door

DEZ
Working, bro

MORRIS
I said…

MORRIS GOES TO DOOR AND OPENS IT
Who are you, man?

HARRISON
Harrison Schwarz, law, finals, almost, my card, gentlemen, heard your stuff, can I interest you in legal representation?

DEZ
Beat it, Harrison

MORRIS
Can you believe this dude, 'copyright specialist'. Suit.

HARRISON
You will need me, gentlemen, time will come.

MORRIS
Beat it, Mr Schwarz

MORRIS AND DEZ CONTINUE THEIR WORK. CHORD PROGRESSIONS. NEARLY THERE. ANOTHER KNOCK. THEY KEEP WORKING. KNOCK AGAIN.

DEZ
Get that, Bro.

MORRIS OPENING DOOR
I said beat it , Harrison

GEORGE
I'll put you chaps down as maybes.
MORRIS AND DEZ RESUME THEIR COMPOSING AT HIGH VOLUME.
THEY DON'T HEAR THE NEXT KNOCK.
HELEN ENTERS. SHE BEGINS HARMONIZING OVER THEIR CHORDS. SOMETHING IS HAPPENING THEY STOP.

MORRIS AND DEZ TOGETHER
Helen

HELEN
Don't stop guys, you have something there. Just add that je ne sais quoi and….
WE HEAR A POST DEMO SONG, GUITAR DEZ, KEYBOARD MORRIS, VOCAL HELEN
BEAT

BACK IN THE CONSULTING ROOM

DOC
You have something there. You really do.

MORRIS
Do you want to dance with me, Doc.
I can see you'd look good on the dance floor.

DOC
Session two tomorrow, Morris Spiegelman. On time, in parameter.

DEZ
Who is it, Moz?

MORRIS
Another suit. What is it with suits and artists?

GEORGE
I expect you guys in the student union this evening. Vote for me, George Lennox for student union president I pledge to ensure…

DEZ
Do we look like we are into politics, George?

MORRIS
Yeah, we're working, good afternoon, George.

GEORGE
Free beer at point of access…

MORRIS
You are so low, George

GEORGE
Thank you, Moz

DEZ
Later, Lennox, like real later

DOC
Went?

MORRIS
We had the sound. It gave us the life.

DOC   Gave?

MORRIS
What's with this. One word day?

DOC
I find your words prelapsarian. There is a before. There will be an after.

MORRIS
Now I'm lost, Doc.

DOC
I want to hear about the incident

MORRIS
The what?

DOC
Yes, the what. You are describing a before, everything led to something, it all went right, it brought you to a place, then. Something, someone, there was Dez, music, Helen, life.

MORRIS
George. Lennox.

DOC
You have spoken of George before

MORRIS
I swore I would never speak to or of him again

DOC
Perhaps you need to

MORRIS
It was a rare evening because I remember where I was – at home. The phone rang…
RING TONE

HELEN ON PHONE
Morris, darling, you watching TV?

MORRIS
Since when do I watch TV?

HELEN
You need to now. Switch it on. Live. News channel.

MORRIS
TO DOC
There is only one weird thing about Helen. She loves the news.

HELEN ON PHONE
News channel, Morris darling. Get on it. I'm calling Schwarz.

HARRISON
ECHO
'Time will come, time will come.'

MORRIS
TO DOC
I don't know what I hate most, TV or lawyers. It was Helen who brought Schwarz in as our suit. Good job, or I assume I wouldn't be able to pay for listening to you, Doc. You know I like Harrison Schwarz really…

DOC
Assumption – from the Latin a taking up, receiving, acceptance.. What did you see on TV, Morris?

MORRIS
Some kind of arena, as big as one of ours, crazy rally, like an apocalypse film, hoards cheering, banners everywhere, projections of Lennox ..
TV ACOUSTIC, SOUND OF THE RALLY FROM THE TV, ROAR OF CROWD BUILDING
FROM STADIUM NOISE ON TV

DJ AS MC

People, this is it, it is what we, the people have all been waiting for.

People say politicians are all the same. This one isn't. He tells it like it is, means what he says, acts on what you, the people really want. He is you.

CROWD NOISE REACHING CRESCENDO

DJ MC

For the people, with the people, power to the people, give it up for Mr George Lennox   MOZ AND DEZ'S HIT IS PLAYED AT FULL VOLUME

ABOVE THE CHEERS

LENNOX

Thank you, folks, thank you

THE MUSIC AND CHEERS CONTINUE

LENNOX BEGINS TO SPEAK

Friends, thank you, and I must say thank you to my mates Dez and Morris for the hit, what times we live in.

Good times but times that could be even better. My friends, we have had enough: EU, UN, IMF, WTO, WFH, WTF I mean how much more do we have to take, it is time to stop the talk, time to be free, time to

THE CROWD ROARS BACK, MORE MUSIC

TV ABRUPTLY SWITCHED OFF. SILENCE.

HELEN ON PHONE
Morris, Morris, you there man, you cool? Look he's a sleazeball politician, Harrison Schwarz will sue him to hell, everything will be alright in the end

MORRIS
It is our music. He used our music. Never asked. Stole it. Used it. Our music.

HELEN ON PHONE
Morris, everything will be alright, there are laws…Morris, Morris
PHONE DISCONTINUED TONE

DOC CONSULTING ROOM ACOUSTIC
DOC
Morris, Mr Spiegelman, breathe

MORRIS
Our music, my music, stole it, for that, fascist, fake, never asked…
CRASH AS MORRIS FALLS

DOC
Morris. ON PHONE Medical assistance please. Possible seizure. Immediate. Consulting room. Dr Voss. Patient: Morris Spiegelman.

5

EXT- DAY OUTSIDE DR VOSS OFFICE
SCHUBERT LIEDER D776 ON THE RADIO HEARD THROUGH OPEN WINDOW TO INT - DR VOSS PREPARES HER NOTES. THEN SWITCHES RADIO OFF AS LIEDER CONCLUDES AND STARTS DICTATATING
HER REPORT INTO LAPTOP BY AUDIO PROGRAMME

DOC
Supervision Report, from Doctor Voss to Director, Cherwell Manor.
Yesterday a critical incident occurred re the treatment of Mr Morris Spiegelman. As lead clinician I am reporting on his progress to date and pathways – possibly unorthodox forward. In view of the treatment to date and the incident leading to hospitalization, however temporary, I propose a …
KNOCK ON HER DOOR
DOC
One moment
SHE CLOSES HER LAPTOP
Enter

DIRECTOR
Good morning, Doctor Voss

DOC
Madam Director, I am composing my supervision report.

DIRECTOR

Confidential within this room of course. However I must ask you about the progress of our Mr Spiegelman.

DOC

May I ask why, Madam Director?

DIRECTOR

You are correct as always Dr Voss to silo clinical and management areas of responsibility. I understood Mr Spiegelman's progress was steady. Now he has been hospitalized.

DOC

Part of the procedure.

DIRECTOR

You intended it?

DOC

I did not intend it. It happened. It may be part of the process

DIRECTOR

Are you speaking retrospectively. You are indicating you have a time line for this client?

DOC

Patients may leave at any time.

DIRECTOR

You do not need to remind me of institute policy. There is however a matter in this case which you as clinician may not be aware. Finance.

DOC

As you put it, that is a discrete area.

DIRECTOR

The funding source – held in an EU jurisdiction – covering Mr Spiegelman's stay with us is not as secure as we initially understood. In three days the funding will shut down. I cannot accept uncovered clients. Policy. I will need results.
If Mr Spiegelman is in your medical opinion not fit to be released from your supervision he will be referred to the public sector.

DOC

Will that be all, madam director?

DIRECTOR (ALREADY LEAVING AS HELICOPTER SOUND OUTSIDE MEANS NEW ARRIVAL)
New clients to greet. I will detain you from your work no longer, Dr Voss.
DIRECTOR EXITS.

DR VOSS RESUMES TYPING, THEN
PICKS UP LANDLINE TELEPHONE

DOC
Switchboard. I will need you to find me some direct line telephone numbers, ex directory no doubt. Thank you. Soon as possible.

6
INT -THE NEXT DAY DR VOSS CONSULTING ROOM

DOC
Good afternoon, Morris, welcome back

MORRIS
If you say so.

DOC
What happened?

MORRIS
Passed out, woke up in hospital, what's new. Problem?

DOC
Passing out, waking up in hospital, I think there might be a problem, don't you Morris?

MORRIS
You know Doc one day you'll make a statement

DOC
One day you'll answer a question.
I ask you again, what happened?

MORRIS
Felt like some drugs, seems the only place I might get some round here is in your hospital. Fat chance.

DOC

I admit I had hoped you would make positive use of the manor's facilities: gardens, pool, refectory, library, common room

MORRIS

Yeah, I decided I'd try the hospital.

DOC

You decided?

MORRIS

Where you going with this, Doc?

DOC

I would like you to leave

MORRIS

You decided? What about me?

DOC

What about you, Morris?   STAND OFF

DOC

As you are still here I am going to ask you to try something

MORRIS

You know me Doc, what you got?

DOC
Imagine

MORRIS
Good keyboard line on it, I'll give you that…

DOC
Imagine you are carrying a black bag up a mountain

MORRIS
I see a trick, didn't expect it of you Dr Ingrid

DOC
Imagine you are carrying a black bag up a mountain. Fill it with grievance, people, things, everything that ever happened against you in your life. Slights, remarks, things people did, things people didn't do. Imagine, the bag, light or heavy, full perhaps, hard to carry,   endless stuff from the past, may be some of it is real, may be some of it isn't. May be there is no difference, may be
It would be simpler, easier, put the bag down,

MORRIS
Put the bag down, make it easier for everyone who..

DOC

You are the one carrying the bag, Morris Spiegelman, what use is it? Imagine, decide, put the bag down, how does it still serve you, you could reach the top without it, the summit, light, put the bag down, empty, simple…

SILENCE DESCENDS IN THE CONSULTING ROOM, MORRIS FALLS ASLEEP. DOC LEAVES HIM THERE.

DOC

CLOSING THE DOOR BEHIND HER

You can leave any time you want, Morris. Cycle away, nothing to carry.

SILENCE EXCEPT FROM THE GARDENS OUTSIDE.

SILENCE OF ENGLISH GARDEN CHANGING TO SOUNDS OF AN IBIZA ISLANDS, CRICKETS, PALM TREES…

7

INT NIGHT – IBIZA CLUB

RHYTHMIC BEAT SOUND INCREASING. AN IBIZA MIX OF THE MOZ AND DEZ ORIGINAL HIT FILLS THE SPACE

DJ INSIDE DEZ HEADPHONES

Phone call for you, Boss

DEZ

This is the zone man, no phone calls

DJ

Some kind of Doctor, calling from England, said you'd want to take it.

DEZ

Keep the sound alive, man, feel me, I'll be right back. I'll take it in my office.   HE LEAVES DANCE HALL. CLOSES DOOR IN HIS OFFICE. THE BEAT SOUND SUBSIDES BUT IS STILL AUDIBLE.

DEZ ON PHONE

Make it quick

DOC

Dez. Dez. I'm sorry that is the only name I have on file. My name is Dr Voss.

DEZ

I don't like files. I don't like Doctors. I'll be late for sunrise, do you know how big a deal that is?

DOC
I apologise for the hour whatever time it is in your zone, I will not keep you. It concerns a patient of mine. Confidential.

DEZ
I don't like secrets. Later, Doc, Peace.

DOC
There is something I would like to put to you. Could you turn the music down?

DEZ No.

DOC
Music comes first, I get that. And money. And trust. And Morris Spiegelman
MUSIC STOPS

8
INT- DR VOSS CONSULTING ROOM
DR VOSS MAKING TEA, SETTING UP CONSULTATION ROOM, WINDOWS OPEN, DISTANT SOUND OF PIANO CHORDS. PIANO STOPS. MORNING BIRDSONG. DOOR OPENS ABRUPTLY

DOC
Good morning, Morris.

MORRIS
Moz will do. Save time. Yes.

DOC
Yes what, Morris?

MORRIS
Yes, the facilities here are cool. I met someone yesterday in the common room. You didn't tell me there was a piano in there.

DOC
Somethings you have to discover for yourself.

MORRIS
Are you being funny?

DOC

Somethings you have to discover for yourself.

MORRIS

A statement. Listen, Doc, I've met someone.

DOC

How nice for you Morris.

MORRIS

I almost preferred the questions

DOC

You want me to ask who did you meet?

MORRIS

A singer, musician, classical but no one is perfect.
Except perfect pitch. Her that is. Rest confidential. You know how it is.

DOC

Tea, Morris?

MORRIS

You must know her, Her name is M-

DOC

Patient, client confidentiality please.

MORRIS
We got talking. We want to do a concert. I am inviting you. I've always had a feeling you love music. Maybe not mine.

DOC
It isn't about my musical tastes

MORRIS
Drop that, you don't have to do that now, I heard of Frank Schubert too , you know, I can learn, I can take in new sounds, we can

DOC
I know you can, so what is new, what do you want me to listen to?

MORRIS
I can't stay for this session, Doc, rehearsals. Charge me for this session of course, actually tomorrow too, You're a pro, you'll understand. I expect we'll be doing the sound check then. Got to split.

DOC (AS MORRIS IS CLOSING DOOR BEHIND HIM) Life isn't a rehearsal. You only come this way once. And other tenets of psychodynamic psychotherapy.

9
INT - RADIO TALK STUDIO
DJ AS HOST , MOZ - DEZ THEME LINE USED AS JINGLE

HOST
People we are live. Live radio doesn't get any better than this. You do not want to touch that dial. It's a changing world, and nothing is changing faster than the music business. Are you starting out in a band or solo in your bedroom, give us a call, are you CEO of a streaming empire, you have my number, you consuming mega hits via subscription services, think you are being ripped off or living it large, I'll give you the number in a mo, first here is your all star panel
From the newsroom in London, if she doesn't know what is going on who does, it is Helen

HELEN
Good to be with you all

HOST
From Ibiza, the party never stops except for this, my man Dez

DEZ
What's happening

HOST
We are going to be hooked up soon as with celebrity lawyer - you heard that those words together - Harrison Schwarz,
Secretary of State, it says here Culture & Media, George Lennox MP - hear the man out - and what a treat, an expert in mental health issues affecting musicians from the Cherwell Manor for R and R.
The number to hit is - hang on to those dials people we are doing The Strand, live news feed from The High Court

HARRISON   ON AIR FEED
…time will come, that musicians, artists will be properly rewarded for their work. This ruling will go down in the textbooks as Schwarz v Lennox
Even as the media landscape changes the principle remains the same, artists own the copyright to their creations, their work cannot be used, exploited, appropriated without express consent, royalties are due to those who compose and perform, time has come.

GEORGE ON AIR
I have known Harrison, Dez and Morris since student days.
Clearly I was erroneous in my belief, held as sincerely as all my beliefs, that I could use their music in the way I did. I am penitent. I own the responsibility.

My position as Secretary of state for Culture and Media is currently untenable. I resign immediately. As a token of my regret at the distress I have caused

I can today announce that all royalties due to Mr Spiegelman will be paid at the request of Mr Schwarz to Cherwell Manor. I have no further comments at this moment except to repeat…

HOST
We are back live in the studio, we are going to open this up in a second, first Helen, news is your area, your reaction to this event. Seismic?

HELEN
Seismic cliché, I could give you others, George is and always has been a first class b…

HOST
This is live radio, Helen

HELEN
If there is any good to come out of this sordid affair it is that Cherwell Manor… HER PHONE IS RINGING

HOST
People, I would prefer your calls come through me…

HELEN

I going to take this, off air, now.   ON HER PHONE Dr Voss. Pleasure. How can I be of assistance?

HOST ON AIR

Dez, you want to come in here?

DOWN THE LINE FROM DEZ, SOUNDS OF CHAMPAGNE BEING OPENED AND IBIZA BEAT MIX OF DEZ AND MOZ STARTING UP

HOST

DEZ, are you on this?

DEZ

Yeah, man, I'm on it….HE FADES OFF AIR.

HOST

Right, talk is talk, music is music. We'll be back after this

DEZ AND MOZ AND HELEN ORIGINAL SONG PLAYED IN ON AIR

IT FADES DOWN AS DOOR CLOSED AND HELEN STEPS INTO CORRIDOR OF STUDIO TO ANSWER PHONE

HELEN ON PHONE

Yes, of course I have heard the news. No, it doesn't alter my position. No, I can't accept your invitation this evening. If I come Morris will not move on. I know that instinctively, I thought you would deduce, Doctor Ingrid. I I don't do regrets. I wish you all, I mean all of you, well. Have a groovy evening.

PHONE OUT

10
INT - EVENING COMMON ROOM OF CHERWELL MANOR
SOUNDS OF FURNITURE BEING SET UP, PIANO TUNED, MICROPHONES CHECKED, SCHUBERT NOTES SUNG BY MARIA AND OTHERS AS VOCAL WARM UP IN PREPARATION FOR CONCERT. PEOPLE COMING IN, HUBBUB BUILDING

DIRECTOR
Dr Voss, this totally your idea? A fraction unorthodox, didn't quite expect it of you. However you have my approval.

DOC
'Wo die Sprache aufhort, fangt die Musik an'

DIRECTOR
'Where the words leave off, music begins.'
You think people who think about money are philistines, Doctor?
Forgive me if I can't stay for the performance, meetings in the margins for me, benefactors, alumni. Oleaginousness would be outside your skillset.   I wish you, all of you, a good evening.

DOC
If you don't want to stay for the music Madam Director why not simply say so?
DIRECTOR LEAVES, FINAL REHEARSAL, VOCAL WARM UPS OPERA STYLE, PIANO CHORDS CFG, AND OTHER SET UP SOUNDS CONTINUE. PIANO CHORDS STOP.

MORRIS

A word, Doc

DOC

Only
one?

MORRIS

Bicycle.

Where did your people park it?

We'll be leaving directly after headliner.

DOC

Your bicycle will be where you locked it, Morris. Why would I move it? Anything else you wish to say, Mr Spiegelman.

MORRIS

I'm glad I put this concert on, Doc. Let's stop talking and get back to music.

APPLAUSE FOR PREVIOUS ACT FADES DOWN

MORRIS

Massive shout out to all those who contributed to this evenings show.

Ladies and Gentlemen, we're going to close with something new not only for Cherwell Manor but a world premiere. On piano, yours truly, on vocals Maria surname confidential,

song I penned called 'Second time is the first time.' Kind of goes like this. 1 2 3 4
MORRIS PLAYS OPENING CHORDS ON THE COMMON ROOM PIANO, MARIA, A CLASSICALLY TRAINED SINGER COMES IN WITH VOCAL LINE.
THE SONG GRADUALLY BUILDS FROM PIANO / VOCAL TO MASSIVE STADIUM ACCOUSTIC, CHEERING CROWDS, THE SONG FULLY ARRANGED MOZ-DEZ STYLE WITH KEYBOARDS, PERCUSSION. MASSIVE HIT, REACHES BIG CHORUS, CHEERS.

MARIA HEARD ON STADIUM STAGES:
Thank you London, oh Vienna, means everything, Copenhagen Vi elsker dig - we love you, thank you Morris.
MORRIS HEARD SAYING ABOVE CROWD Dez on beats, Maria on vocal, shout out.
CHEERING FADES.   SILENCE.

11
EXT- THE GARDEN SOUNDS OF CHERWELL MANOR

DOC

Thank you for meeting me gentlemen. Don't take this the wrong way but I hope I never see you again. Here.

DEZ

No worries, Doctor Ingrid.

HARRISON

Time always comes, Doctor Voss

GULL CAR DOORS CLOSING. THEY GLIDE DOWN THE MANOR DRIVE IN THEIR ELECTRIC CAR

CODA

DOC EXT -INT

WALKING BACK TO HER CONSULTING ROOM

DOC

You can tell much about people by how they leave.

Morris? Did he totally know what happened? Cycled off without a thank you?

It is my profession to facilitate departures. Wouldn't have it any other way. Lyrics and words are not the same. 'Second time around is the first.' A coded thank you?

Schwarz's office did courier me tickets for the MDM Morris Dez Maria concert in Vienna. Note to self: investigate citation of humorous ironic intervention in psychodynamics? SHE IS BACK IN HER OFFICE. SWITCHES ON RADIO. OPENS WINDOW. THE SCHUBERT LIEDER IS OVERPOWERED BY HELICOPTER DEPARTURE. SHE CLOSES WINDOW.

AS SOUND OF HELICOPTER SUBSIDES SHE OPENS WINDOW AGAIN. SOUNDS OF GARDEN. SOUND OF HER AUDIO TYPING

'Morris Spiegelman is alright.'

/

Principal location: Cherwell Manor, the present

\

CAST

Morris Spiegelman

Dez   (Devasilpa)

Director, Cherwell Manor

Harrison Schwarz

George Lennox

Helen

DJ / MC / Radio host

Maria

/

Morris Spiegelman is Alright

John F King © 2023

ISBN 978-1-8383426-3-0

Also in this series from   York Europe Publications:

Prog 2015
ISBN 978-0-9931306-0-1

www.johnkinginternational.co.uk

Prog II Part 2

Variations on a musical theme:

Les Musiciens

Soft Machine

Song Cycle

Review – *Different Trains*
From www.secondgeneration.org.uk

Bibliography

Les Musiciens

They called the district Les Musiciens before I moved here. Now of course saves them renaming it. I wouldn't live anywhere else. Iggy Berlin, Stones London, L A Doors, me Nice. That's the way I like it.
That's the way I want it to stay.
I walk to work every day I work. If I'm not in the studio I'm by the sea, ideas come to me in waves. Rue Berlioz is fantastic, my villa, the Faust, not as predictable as you might expect.
This cat has set himself up on the corner of Rue Karr. Main chancer.
Nothing wrong with that. I'd do the same if I had to   – again. Street contact keeps you on it.
I drop him a few euros if I've had a good day before   I hit Le Koncept for a cursory Kir.
He doesn't know who I am.
I expect he'll move on soon enough. Move on up, give up or make it. If he asks me for advice I'll give it, naturally, but if there is one thing I learned on my road is people have to do it their way.   It goes on for longer than I expected, him gigging on the corner I mean. I could see – hear – why it wasn't happening for him. Eventually I couldn't stop myself. He nodded to me once when I was enroute for Le Koncept. I think it was a nod, it wasn't particularly rhythmic. Usually he was gone when I was walking back to rue Berlioz. Yeah, I may have been staying longer in the bar, the Kirs becoming precursors for something else.
'It's your singing, man,' I said. 'you're off the beat, not in a good way.'
The nodding stopped, no not rhythmic.
I was walking from the Villa to the Koncept every day now – I'd looped out the studio detour, why waste time?

One evening, he missed a beat.

'You ok, man?' He said.

I liked his speaking voice. I felt it was down to me as the older man and evidently fellow English gent to re-establish contact.

I'd kept the recording engineers on standby – you never know when the muse will return. 'Let me show you something, or rather I want you to hear something,' I said.

His guitar case was full of euros. He looked at me closely.

I smiled: 'you think I'm interested in a flight case of euros?' He didn't answer.

I offered him a beer from the studio ice box. He declined.

'Cool set up you have here, man,' He said. 'Shame you not using your time wisely.' The impertinence threw me.

'Hit it,' I said to the duty engineer. He flicked a row of switches, the sound filled the room. He nodded and tapped to the timing. The track stopped.

He stopped. I filled the silence.

'Well?'

'You sing well,' he said.

'But.'

'Do you mind?' he said, gesturing to the engineer. We played the track once more, laying in his guitar.

'One more time,' he said to the engineer, directly. He played the piano in the corner of the studio. I hadn't noticed it before.

The other sound engineers rematerialized.

After the track there was silence.

The lead engineer broke it.

'He's got it,' she said, 'you've got it.' I understood why the area was named with a plural.

Sometimes he comes down from Cimiez and we have an ice tea at the Koncept. A girl sings along to a boogie box on the corner of Alphonse Karr. We don't have time to stop.

Prog II
From *Nice People* 2018 ISBN 978-0-9931306-6-3

Soft Machine

Mid life now,

Listening to the first album I ever bought.   Forced to bec‹ a teacher 'cos I couldn't play piano like their keyboard player,

You know, the guy who wore sunglasses even in Ronnie's basement at 3 a m.

First girlfriend hated them, only made me like'em even more,

Loved her still, still do,

Even though we broke up before the band did, musical differences.

What was their first (and only) single – 3 minutes,
I mean, that's longer than…yeah, yeah right…
Reached 99 in the Melody Maker top 100
Cool, wouldn't want a sell out, I mean would we , man.
Only *I* get it of course.

Time signatures as crazy as the times
   13/4
17/8

Johan Strauss I don't think so!
   Got F – ed up, Funked up that is, 1978 I think it was
Same as me. We all did. Nothing wrong in that.
Started dancing again in the 90s. Different girl, different time signature – ¾

Dancing classes in the window less hall.
Funny,

Guy there, one of these people you can't make out how old they are.

Waltzes in, dances to his own tune.
   Never takes his sunglasses off though, all evening.
Funny that….

In the windowless hall, in the middle of the evening, in the middle of the year, in the   middle of…

Soft Machine also featured in *Wise Guy and other fables*
2008
ISBN 978-0-9558519-0-2

Song Cycle

Centre stage darkness illuminated by approach of offstage car headlights showing **CONSTANCE** *a derelict but retains a hint of a life before, asleep by the overflowing clothes bin in a recycling centre adjacent supermarket. Swish of electric car, brakes, stops.*
Click of boot and side door opening, **ELLEN**'s *shoes on gravel.*
ELLEN *voice off* Clothes like this. The past, the time before, no one needs them now.
ELLEN off, throws bag at the clothes bin. ELLEN doesn't wait to see where bag lands. As doors closing
ELLEN 'Drive on' *to chauffeur, off. Car and lights move away. Bag into view.*
CONSTANCE awakened by voice and bag landing next to her observes but doesn't think it worth moving. It is dawn, centre stage light gradually up. CONSTANCE settles again as car fades to silent.

She is awakened by a theme mobile telephone ring tone. At first CONSTANCE is disorientated and cannot locate the sound but it is coming from the suit bag. **ELLEN** *voice as Ansa phone message clicks in* Ellen Gold, International Artists Management, contact via Zoom. Leave a message if you can't.

Beep. Off.
Phone rings again, same message. CONSTANCE isn't going to get any more sleep. Stirs herself, rummages, ascertains there must be a phone among the clothes bags. Message again. Listens to message. Intrigued. She locates the sound as from the suit bag. Notes and begins to unzip branded bag. Stops and turns to face out. Light continually rising. It eventually becomes a spotlight.

CONSTANCE

How dare you judge me? You think it couldn't happen to you, think again. I was someone once. Someone real, someone who existed, an artiste. Yes. I was, am. Appearances. That's the past. The time before. Time before it stopped. If your life curved up again when the graph went down I'm pleased for you. Really. Excuse me.

She turns back to the suit bag. Unzips it and examines it. Begins to extract the clothes within. Lays clothes out. It is a formal suit for classical concerts. She begins to get dressed as for a performance, tentatively then with more confidence as she dresses hums ['Vissi d'arte..']

CONSTANCE *speaking as she puts on the clothes directly over her rags.*

You think it couldn't happen to you, think again. Didn't the crisis bring what was going to happen anyway. It only happened for me sooner. Maybe I had further to fall than you did?

She locates the phone in the inside pocket of the jacket. Message. Presses a button. It plays the music as she is on hold **ELLEN** *recorded Ansa phone message* You are in a queue. Your time will come.

CONSTANCE Zoom, what's that? I always did things face to face. That's how I started. That's what finished me. The concert halls were emptying before they became empty. People had been at home too long. They forgot to come out again.

ELLEN *phone message* You are in a queue, your time will come.

CONSTANCE *is now almost fully dressed. Reads out the business card from top of jacket pocket 'EGI Artist Management.' Fully dressed her old form is emerging.* This must have been meant to happen. There must be a reason. There has to be. It isn't over until… *The hold theme music stops. There is a beep. CONSTANCE is on. She takes a drink from a bottle and begins to sing into phone as microphone*

Beep / Fade

Song Cycle also available in:
ISBN 978-1-8383426-1-6
York Europe Publication   *Micro Waves II*   2022
J F King
©

AUDIO REVIEW for *Second Generation Voices / ProgII*
Steve Reich's Different Trains: Minimalism and Memory
The Listening Service, BBC Sounds bbc.co.uk
'After Auschwitz to write a poem is barbaric…'
Theodor Adorno *Cultural Criticism and Society* 1949 This quotation is cited at the outset of this thoughtful and moving radio essay on the musical composition *Different Trains* by Steve Reich. Speaking in 2011 the composer said 'if anyone came to me and said we would like you to write a piece about The Holocaust I would run in the opposite direction as fast as possible. It is a horrendous idea. I would be totally unequipped to do it.'
However the eminent musicologist Richard Taruskin stated '*Different Trains* is the only adequate musical response to The Holocaust.' It is a 'life changing testimony, a confrontation with the genocide.' In this 29-minute podcast BBC Radio Three broadcaster Tom Service presents an acute examination of this work and the wider question of representations of The Holocaust through the arts. *Different Trains* for string quartet with amplification, speech phasing and tape was premiered in the USA by the Kronos quartet in 1988.

\

There are three movements:

1   America before the war. Here the string quartet accelerates the rhythm of trains as experienced by Reich as a boy moving between east and west coast USA in 1940. Spoken word is looped against the violas. The composer is reflecting how different trains were taking children to darker destinations across the European continent.

2   Europe during the war. Voices from Holocaust survivors from the archive of Yale University are programmed into the musical notes and rhythms and the sounds of sirens.

3   After the war. The US and European *sprechstimme* achieve a total fusion connecting memories and musical echoes freeing all the lost voices.   After introducing the music and its compositional context Service surveys other pieces that memorialise the horror more directly, notably Schoenberg *A Survivor from Warsaw* Op 46 1947, Shostakovich and Yevtushenko Symphony 13 *Babi Yar* Op 113 1941 and Górecki Symphony 3 *Symphony of Sorrowful Songs* Op36 1976.

As expert witness Jonathan Freedland, author of *Jacob's Gift* and *The Escape Artist: The Man Who Broke Out of Auschwitz to Warn the World*   is called to enter the debate on how the arts have approached The Holocaust. Indeed is it wrong for the arts to consider this evil event at all, perhaps the only response is silence.

Freedland's guiding principle is 'stick to the facts.' His leading quartet is *The Diary of Anne Frank* 1947, Lanzmann *Shoah* 1985, Levi *If this is a Man* 1947 and Spielberg *Schindler's List* 1994. There is some discussion of introducing comedic effect in Benigni *Life is Beautiful* 1997 and adding fictional devices as in Boyne *The Boy in the Striped Pyjamas* 2006.   Now we move from memory (First Generation) to history how will these meditations change; will imagination fill the void left by witness?

This concise programme of reflection and analysis concludes that Steve Reich's unique composition is an eloquent and responsible solution to this artistic and historical challenge.

As the voices and strings fade we may think of Aldous Huxley's most apt description:
'After silence that which comes nearest to expressing the inexpressible is music…we are grateful to the artist, especially the musician, for saying clearly what we have aways felt, but never able to express.'
Music at Night 1931
Second Generation Network
2023
www.secondgeneration.org.uk

www.johnkinginternational.co.uk

Also by **John F King** at

York Europe Publishing:

Wise Guy and other fables, 2008   ISBN 978-0-955851902
   Wise Guy, 2012, is also available as an eBook at Smashwords ISBN 9781476351735   *_Drama King_ I 2010
ISBN 978-0-955851919
Funky / Guy and other micro-fiction, 2012   ISBN 978-0-955851964
Micro-Waves, 2012
ISBN 978-0-955851933   **Vienna,**
Love, 2014
ISBN 978-0-955851971   Write

Coach, 2014
ISBN 978-0-955851988
Write Coach **II** 2015
ISBN 978-0-9931306-1-8
A and E 2014   ISBN 978-0-955851995
Prog 2015
ISBN 978-0-9931306-0-1

What's Left 2016
ISBN 978-0-993106-2-5

Low – Rise 2016
ISBN 978-0-9931306-3-2
SW10 2017
ISBN 978-09931306-4-9
West End Story 2018
ISBN 978-0-993106-5-6
Nice People 2018   ISBN 978-0-99331306-6-3
Memories of the Future 2019   ISBN 978-09931306-7-0
4 x 4 2020
ISBN 978-0-9931306-8-7
Drama King II 2020
ISBN 978-1-716354335   **Super-Over** 2021
ISBN 978-1-8383426-0-9

Micro-waves II 2022

ISBN 978-1-8383426-2-3   York Europe Publishing
  Prog II 2023 by John F King   ISBN 978-1-8383426-3-0   www.johnkinginternational.co.uk

/

www.ingramcontent.com/pod-product-compliance
Lightning Source LLC
Chambersburg PA
CBHW081602040426
42450CB00014B/3307